THE WORLD
THERE IS NO
PLANET B

THINGS YOU CAN DO RIGHT NOW
TO SAVE OUR PLANET

LOUISE BRADFORD

summersdale

SAVE THE WORLD

An Hachette UK Company
www.hachette.co.uk

Summersdale Publishers Ltd
Part of Octopus Publishing Group Limited
Carmelite House
50 Victoria Embankment
LONDON
EC4Y 0DZ
UK

www.summersdale.com

Printed and bound in the Czech Republic

Printed on 100% recycled card and paper

ISBN: 978-1-78783-034-9

CONTENTS

INTRODUCTION

Overwhelming evidence suggests that our planet is facing an unprecedented threat. Our weather is unpredictable and can be dangerous to human life; there are flash floods and increasing polarities of heat and cold. Plastic litter can be seen every day, on our beaches, in our rivers and tangled in plants and trees; more worrying still, the microplastics that fill our seas are harming our wildlife, upsetting the delicate balance of sensitive ecosystems and entering our food chain.

What we produce for our own convenience is not rotting away or magically disappearing when it is no longer needed; it is clogging up our ecology and harming all the living things that share this planet with us. And all the other ways in which human activity is choking our planet – the burning of fossil fuels, unsustainable logging and intensive agriculture, to name just three – have now become **impossible to ignore**.

What we believed about the environmental impact of human life as little as a decade ago has now changed, and we face a doubly complex issue. First, we need to clean up the mess we've already made, recognizing and then dealing with the pollution that already exists. Second, there is an increasing urgency to change how we act, so the problem does not get any worse – to stop further thoughtless and irresponsible human actions. This requires clever and innovative thinking, which can feel unattainable as it threatens to disrupt established ways of living which until now we have rather taken for granted. But **change is possible**. Saving the planet can sound like a daunting task; something that feels just too large and too difficult to fix. Yes, governments and corporations need to do their bit, but if we are to save the planet, **we must all take action** and we should not underestimate the impact that individual changes can make.

It's time to stop, think and then take action. This book is here to empower you to make changes, large and small, in both your attitudes and actions. Some of the ideas within are simple changes that take seconds and will benefit both you and the environment for years to come; others are ongoing things that need to be repeated and integrated into our lifestyles to ensure that we reap the long-term rewards. But the best thing to do is to begin. What if you were to start somewhere? What if everyone did the same? Changing your personal practices to support the planet can begin as a small endeavour, but will grow and flourish to become a larger part of your life, enabling you to take back control of what can feel like the insurmountable problem of environmental damage. By instigating steps to address the harm we do personally to our planet, we can set an example for those who know us, who may also start to do things differently. In that quiet way, through the collective accumulation of thousands and even millions of individuals taking ownership of their personal environmental impact, the change in habits that is so badly needed can come to pass.

We all have consumer habits drilled into us over decades, so adapting to any change may take a while, but if **we keep trying to innovate and to challenge the status quo**, the fad of environmentalism will soon become mainstream. Psychologists believe it takes at least three weeks for us to form a habit, so why not try a few of the practices in this book for that amount of time, then review your progress and try a few more? You will gain momentum and the planet will benefit.

It's not always easy to be green, to alter approaches we have followed unthinkingly for years, which can seem fundamental to how our society functions. But it is possible! The key is in educating ourselves and others, finding new ways to do things that we've previously taken for granted and taking action to **allow the planet to heal and to prosper**.

HOME

The word "ecology" derives from the Greek word *oikos* meaning "house, home or place to live", so it is apt to start with some eco-friendly actions that you could utilize in the home. The home is a place where environmental endeavours can extend from a few simple actions to a wider lifestyle choice. It's your decision what you do in your own home and how far you want to change, but this chapter should give you some simple ideas on where to start.

ENERGY EFFICIENCY IN THE HOME

One of the easiest ways to start your eco-friendly journey is by tackling inefficient or unnecessary energy use. The burning of gas, oil and coal for heat and electricity is the largest single source of global greenhouse-gas emissions, so the key to reducing the burden of climate change is to switch to green alternatives, to find ways to reduce our energy use and to make it more efficient.

Light Bulbs

Energy-efficient light bulbs are now commonplace, with most countries banning the use of incandescent ones. If you haven't already got energy-efficient light bulbs installed, switch to compact fluorescent lamps (CFLs) or light-emitting diodes (LEDs) which typically use between 25 and 80 per cent less energy than traditional incandescents.

Lights

Turn lights off when you leave a room. If your budget allows, invest in timers and sensors so that lights are not unnecessarily powered.

Don't Standby

Do not leave appliances on standby; electronic devices kept in standby mode account for up to 10 per cent of residential power use. This applies to anything that's plugged in – TVs, laptops, chargers and even toasters – although we don't recommend unplugging your fridge!

Efficient Washing

Only run a dishwasher or washing machine when it's full – see Laundry on p.19 for further tips.

Low Power

Use low power mode on your phone or laptop. The less power you use, the less electricity you will consume in recharging your device.

Save Water

Only boil the water that is needed for a cup of tea, not a kettleful.

Home Energy Sources

Traditional energy sources for the home rely on the established infrastructure of the electricity grid and, within that framework, suppliers who provide the energy. In order to heat our homes and cook our food, most of us use gas or oil, both of which deplete fossil fuels (fossil fuel is a general term for buried combustible geologic deposits).

One of the simplest steps you can take is to ask your supplier if they have a renewable energy provision and switch to it if they do. If not, look for another supplier that can offer wind, solar, geothermal or another renewable source of energy, or at least one that offers part-renewable options, investing profits into renewable sources.

Keeping Your Home Warm (Part 1)

Heating our homes accounts for around 70 per cent of all residential energy use. Even turning your thermostat down by a single degree can save a huge amount on your energy bill. Homes which are effectively insulated use less energy, so by making your home as efficient as possible, not only will you be saving the planet, you'll be saving on bills too.

 Switch lightweight curtains for thick, lined ones to keep in more heat, and keep them open during the day to let in free heat, from the sun.

 Use draught excluders under doors and windows to prevent heat from escaping; old-style doors and windows (particularly single pane) are the most common offenders.

 Add self-adhesive rubber seals to any doors, windows or cracks to prevent heat getting out.

Put radiator reflectors behind any radiators you have in your home to make sure as much heat as possible is reflected back into the room (rather than into the wall).

 Move furniture away from radiators to allow the heat to circulate effectively.

 Check the insulation on your hot-water tank and upgrade it if necessary; it can save you hundreds every year.

 Use (or install) timers so that the heating only comes on at the times it is most needed. Setting your heating to come on low about half an hour before you wake up is more efficient than turning it on high in an effort to quickly heat a chilly house when you get up.

Invest in more blankets and throws to keep yourself warm, rather than relying on heating.

 Keep yourself warm by applying the same principles as those who live and work in the world's coldest climates: wear a base layer of cotton, silk or wool, a mid layer of fleece or light wool and a top-layer jumper or waterproof windcheater.

Keeping Your Home Warm (Part 2)

There are also some bigger-picture things you could consider, should your budget allow. These tips cost more upfront, but will benefit you, and the planet, in the long run.

 Sustainable energy sources, such as solar panels, wind turbines, ground-source heat pumps, air-source heat pumps, biomass pellet burners and stoves, can be considered and installed in the home. If it is feasible, switch to one or more of these options.

 Underfloor heating is more energy-efficient than wall-mounted radiators.

 Home insulation (especially insulation using eco-friendly materials which are natural or recycled), particularly in cavity walls and roofs, will retain heat, reducing the need for energy-sapping consumption. If you want to try DIY options (such as reusing old curtains or other old materials) check first that these are fireproof and check out helpful tutorials online before attempting your own insulations.

 Double- or even triple-glazed windows or sealed window units retain heat and are the most effective when it comes to being eco-friendly. Window units which contain inert gases (argon, krypton or xenon) minimize the conduction of heat. If this is out of your budget, there are DIY options to seal up and reinforce old windows to make them more efficient at retaining heat.

Laundry

What are your laundry habits? Most clothes do not need to be washed after every single wear, and contrary to popular belief, washing clothes only when they need a clean will not make you dirty or unhygienic. Better still, you'll be doing the environment a favour at the same time.

Famously, the CEO of Levi Strauss & Co. asserted in 2014 that to achieve sustainability, purchasers of his company's iconic jeans should stop washing them. It's reported he didn't wash his own jeans for a year! Excessive laundry leads to the high consumption of water, energy, detergents and solvents. Hand-washing clothes uses a far smaller volume of water (and obviously less electricity) than machine-washing. Ironing too requires electricity. Give each stage of the laundry process a rethink: are you being as energy- and water-efficient as you could be? Here are some basic tips for saving the world as you wash your clothes:

Use eco-programmes on your appliances.

Wash at a cooler temperature; 30 degrees is sufficient for most cleaning and uses far less energy.

 Consider using a micro-fibre catchment bag to lessen water pollution (see Manmade Textiles, p.131).

 Use eco-balls – these are balls you add to your wash which use friction and small long-lasting pellets to shake dirt out of the fabrics.

 Consider using soap nuts instead of chemical detergents; they are all-natural and therefore very safe and kind to the environment (and your non-chemically washed clothes will be kinder to your skin), though they do require hot water to work properly, so they may not be for everyone.

 Don't wash half loads. Wait and wash a full load.

If buying a new washing machine, look for one with at least an A rating for energy efficiency, check that it comes with an eco- or low-temperature setting, look for water-efficient models and, unless you have a large family with lots of regular laundry, consider buying a smaller model as machines are more efficient if they run with a full load.

 Use concentrated detergent which is environmentally friendly, or make your own out of soap granules and bicarbonate of soda, following preparation recipes online.

 Avoid clothes and other fabrics which require dry-cleaning, a process which, due to chemical use, is notoriously bad for the planet. If you must dry-clean, send metal hangers and plastic sheeting back to the dry-cleaners to be reused.

 If you must tumble-dry, ensure the machine's lint filter is cleaned out on a regular basis. A clogged lint filter can extend drying time considerably.

LINE DRYING

There are fewer simpler pleasures than a sunny day, a light breeze, and a garden with laundry hanging on the line to dry. Even in a damp climate, it's possible for clothes to dry outside and allowing them to do so pays dividends, environmentally speaking. We also know that tumble-drying can alter the fibres in your clothes and sheets, causing fade and shrinkage. Tumble-drying uses a lot of electricity: the average household dryer programme uses just over 4 kWh of energy and produces around 1.8 kg (4 lb) of CO_2. If every household with a tumble-dryer dried even one load of laundry outside each week, instead of by machine, collectively they would save over a million tonnes of CO_2 in the UK alone every year.

BATTERIES

Batteries, which are used in a myriad of appliances and toys, contain chemicals considered to be toxic, such as lead, nickel, lithium and mercury. After being discarded, batteries are sent to landfill, but in the course of breaking down (a process of approximately 100 years) the chemicals they contain leach into the soil and the water system, causing contamination. Using rechargeable batteries goes some way to arresting this environmentally negative process, as batteries are no longer thrown away when they have run out. These batteries can be recharged between 500 and 1,000 times and will last for two to three years.

All batteries, including rechargeable ones, can be recycled at specific recycling points, with some supermarkets having battery recycling buckets for this purpose. So rather than throwing batteries out with your normal rubbish, keep them aside and recycle in bulk. Alternatively, think twice before using any appliance that is battery-powered.

CLEANING

Most store-bought cleaning products are full of chemicals which wash away into the drains and could end up in the water cycle. They're also often packaged in single-use plastic, which at the very least should be recycled where possible, but can be avoided altogether if you make your own. Here are some quick and simple tips to eco up your cleaning routine.

Make Your Own

Make your own cleaning products and bottle them in old, cleaned-out glass or plastic containers or in reuse bottles with mechanical, plastic spray attachments for any homemade cleaners you want to spray onto surfaces.

Washing Powder

Washing powder can be made at home using grated bars of soap and bicarbonate of soda.

Surface Cleaner

Surface cleaner can be made using vinegar or lemon juice, adding eucalyptus or tea tree oil for a freshening scent.

Cleaning Cloths

Reuse cleaning cloths or use old clothes cut into rags instead of disposable kitchen towels or single-use wipes.

Washing-Up Liquid

Use eco-friendly washing-up liquid or make your own washing-up liquid from lemon juice or vinegar.

Brushes And Scourers

Buy and use sustainably produced dish brushes and scourers, such as those made of wood or bamboo rather than plastic.

Kitchen Roll

In recent years, disposability has come to be synonymous with ease and cleanliness, principles which we now need to challenge if we are to achieve environmental sustainability. Kitchen roll is a stalwart of most households. The production of paper kitchen roll uses up millions of trees and billions of gallons of water before we even get to the impact of transportation in distribution and supply. After a single use the paper towel becomes disposable mush decomposing in a landfill site. But there are better alternatives, such as old rags or cloths that can be washed and reused. Try cutting up old cotton T-shirts for this purpose and having a basket of them within easy reach in the kitchen. Use for mess and splashes, and launder to reuse. Do this for a few weeks to ingrain the new habit. Alternatively, buy eco-cloths in bulk and reuse them instead of using paper towels. High-fibre eco-cloths are made primarily of a highly absorbent manmade polyester fabric, so they don't meet all eco-credentials, but the assumption is that they will be used again and again, which goes some way to mitigating their environmental impact.

BUYING IN BULK

There is an economy to buying in bulk; buying large containers of food and cosmetics to decant, rather than buying many small containers, is cheaper and more environmentally sound, thanks to the huge reduction in disposable packaging. If it works for you, why not considering buying in bulk with friends or housemates, to share the benefits?

REFILLERIES

Start to use "refilleries", if they are available to you, where you bring your own containers to fill and take home (even some supermarkets offer this for certain produce), or where you purchase and use the supplied (and generally eco-friendly) containers and then return with them for refills. This simple concept was common in the past, but as convenience became our expectation, we ceased to use this method.

MILK ROUNDS

If you drink milk on a regular basis, consider going back to an old-fashioned milk round, using glass milk bottles which are returned when empty and refilled.

DON'T OVERBUY

There are some drawbacks to bulk buying which you need to consider if the environmental gains aren't to be offset by various kinds of losses. For instance, the upfront costs are higher, and some foods do not store well, so make sure you don't overbuy food that will end up being thrown out.

Responsible Decluttering

Decluttering our homes and minimal living have been hailed in recent years as a way to reap psychological and physical benefits from streamlined living. While donating unwanted items to charity has been encouraged and is far better than throwing things away or taking large items to the dump, the better solution would be to avoid acquiring these things in the first place. This comes down to changing our shopping habits (see p.125), but in the meantime, if you do need to declutter, think carefully along the following lines about how you dispose of unwanted items:

 Which charities will benefit most from a donation? Do they actually need this product? Would they be able to resell it?

 Do you know anyone who might want or need what you discard? A child might have grown out of something that would perfectly fit a friend's child, or perhaps someone else might be looking for a bookcase exactly like the one you want to get rid of.

It's not just charity shops that could do with unwanted goods; refugee programmes happily accept unwanted shoes, clothes, tents, sleeping bags, food, mobile phones and more. Check to see if there's a local donation point near you.

 Donate with thought; there are organizations which channel items to the right recipients, such as prams for new mothers, or smart clothes for those recommencing paid work after a period of homelessness, or blankets for animal shelters, etc.

 Books accumulated over a lifetime may be one area of clutter that requires a keen eye and a strong nerve to reduce in number. Donate books you no longer need to non-profit organizations which in turn direct them to more needy recipients such as schools, charities, prisons and hospitals.

 Unwanted books and magazines are often gratefully received at doctors' or dentists' offices, to keep in the waiting rooms.

In The Bathroom

The bathroom is a powerhouse of energy and water consumption – a bad bathroom could be wasting tonnes of water, using up energy on inefficient heating rails and flushing all kinds of chemicals and microplastics down the drains. But an eco-friendly bathroom is both easy to create and incredibly satisfying to use. Here are our top tips:

Watch out for products which contain sodium laureth sulphate, parabens, petroleum by-products and synthetic microbeads, which not only have an environmental impact when flushed into our water system but are also suspected to be dangerous to humans, as they contain carcinogens. Buy and apply with a conscience; ask yourself if you wish to put such chemicals on your hair and skin, when the risks are to some extent unknown.

31

Use bars of soap rather than liquid soap that comes in plastic dispensers.

 Buy shampoo, conditioner and shower-gel bars, rather than plastic-packaged liquid alternatives.

 Wash your hair less. Shampoo contains parabens, sulphates and other chemicals which enter the water system through our drains. Human hair is perfectly capable of regulating its own cleanliness without the use of shampoos and conditioners. You could try rinsing it with apple cider vinegar, which rebalances the natural oils in the hair or, to reduce your environmental impact, simply opt to wash it only once a week.

 Avoid aerosol deodorants, which have been proven to adversely affect climate; consider rock salt or stick deodorants instead.

For women, the use of a menstrual cup negates the need for disposable sanitary products.

 Switch to toothpaste tablets, which can be bought in refillable, reusable containers, rather than having to throw away a plastic toothpaste tube every time.

 Use safety razors with recyclable blades, rather than disposing of the entire thing after a few uses.

 Opt for bamboo toothbrushes, as these are recyclable or compostable, rather than plastic ones, which are not.

 Use natural scourers such as loofahs instead of synthetic ones.

 Use washable cotton pads or face cloths instead of disposable cotton wool or single-use face wipes.

Buy a single large tub of coconut oil for moisturizing, wiping away make-up, conditioning your hair and for use in homemade scrubs rather than buying individually packaged items for each application.

 If you must use cotton buds, opt for ones made of paper not plastic.

 Try henna dye blocks, rather than home hair-dye kits that come with unnecessary plastic bottles, cardboard boxes, plastic trays and gloves, and sometimes even plastic tools.

 We all accept that toilet paper is something we can't do without! But we can use a recycled, eco-friendly version.

 Open the window rather than switching on the extractor fan.

BATHROOM CLEANING

Use environmentally friendly and non-toxic bathroom cleaners as well as reusable cleaning implements such as cloths or sponges, which can be hygienically washed, rather than disposable wipes, which cannot. Our habit of using disinfectant chemicals to achieve high levels of hygiene in toilet spaces also comes at a price; and don't forget that the same levels of cleanliness and disinfection are achievable using hot, soapy water and elbow grease.

Making Your Own

It's easy to make DIY versions of most beauty products, relying on a few bathroom or kitchen staples and avoiding the need to buy anything packaged in plastic. A simple exfoliating scrub can be made quickly by mixing coconut oil and sugar, or you could look online for more complex recipes that call for essential oils, honey, eggs and other store-cupboard products you probably already have lying around.

AN ECO-HOME

Finally, one of the most effective things we can do to make sure our homes are eco-friendly is to utilize all areas of innovative environmental thinking when building new homes. If you are buying a home, see where you can install environmentally conscious options and gain a full understanding of the environmental credentials of the home you are buying. Where possible consider standard elements, such as the supply of energy, and what kind of heating the house will use, and rather than simply coming to a decision based on price, base your energy-sourcing decisions instead on the environment and an assessment of the carbon footprint you will generate. And if you're lucky enough to be building a home to your own designs, the options for incorporating environmentally friendly elements are huge – you could look into sourcing sustainable or recycled materials, installing solar panels, state-of-the-art insulation and water-harvesting solutions.

FOOD

The vast majority of us take our food for granted. We buy what we want when we want, and rarely do we consider its provenance, how it has been produced and packaged, how our choice of food and food provider impact the environment, or what happens to the 20 to 40 per cent of all household food that ends up thrown away – often still inside the packaging – destined to rot in landfill. However, luckily there are endless ways we can help to make positive changes and still enjoy delicious, healthy and nutritious food. Read on!

WHERE TO SHOP

Part of the process of making planet-friendly choices is to give your custom to those retailers who share your environmental values. This may mean questioning the largest and most established retailers; economies of scale mean they often buy their produce from the large-scale industrial farms that are a major source of global emissions, so the large retailers may be the worst offenders. There is value to be had in seeking out suppliers who make decision-making easier for you by routinely offering low- or no-plastic options, or at least pledging to work toward that goal.

VEG BOXES

See if a local farmer provides a vegetable box service. Or find a national company that grows centrally but delivers locally. Seasonal vegetable boxes enable us to cook a wider repertoire of food, to be more innovative with our ingredients and to cook produce that is in surplus rather than scarcity.

BUY LOCAL

Instead of buying from a large out-of-town supermarket, requiring a car journey that uses fuel, try buying locally from a market and walking there, if possible. Take a trolley or a bike with panniers if you have too much to carry. As well as cutting your own transport use, you'll also be supporting local suppliers and smaller companies, rather than giving your money to large stores whose practices and policies are often questionable.

BUY ECO

Choose a shop that supports the environment. Lots of small groceries, bakeries or wholefood sellers implement eco-friendly systems such as donating just-expired food to local foodbanks or to the homeless, composting waste, avoiding plastic packaging, refusing to sell products that contain palm oil, and offering staff or customer initiatives such as discounts if you cycle to the store or bring your own cotton tote bags. We should all be supporting and promoting this kind of activism!

Provenance

These days, there is so much on offer in our shops! So long as we demand such extensive selections of food, retailers will continue to provide a surplus. If we keep buying it, they'll keep supplying it!

It's hard to appreciate how many separate processes have taken place to put a salad or a sandwich in front of you, and certainly the convenience factor cannot be disregarded. But when you really consider where your food has come from, the environmental impact it's having becomes crystal clear.

The most obvious sign is the country of origin, which is usually stated on most fresh food. Have those vegetables been imported from halfway around the world, depriving the local community of food in order to feed our appetites? Has that pack of meat been driven thousands of miles to reach the shelf? Even if it's not labelled, common sense will tell you whether the item is local and in season – do those berries really look like they were grown in your local area? We all know what our local climate and landscapes allow for us realistically to grow, so if it's not something your great-grandparents would have recognized, it's probably not local.

Buying locally produced food not only reduces the transport requirements it took for the food to reach you (the carbon footprint of shipping or lorry transports for foods is vast), but often also means less plastic, as longer transport times require more robust packaging. Compare a paper bag of fruit from a local pick-your-own farm to fruit that is shipped in plastic wrapping or punnets, often with multiple packs shrink-wrapped in plastic, inside cardboard boxes or more plastic, with all those labels and shipping documents.

If cooking a recipe that relies on out-of-season or obscure ingredients that aren't locally available, look for alternatives: there are often local options that will give a similar flavour, texture or consistency to a recipe, without contributing to the world's carbon emissions.

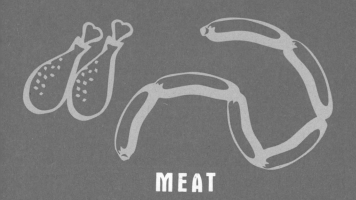

MEAT

Some of you aren't going to like this one. But here's the simple truth: one of the biggest single changes you can make if you want to help save the world, is to cut out meat. Scientists agree that if we want to let our world recover from all the damage we've already put it through, we will have to drastically reduce our meat consumption, globally.

Although it's only the fourth or fifth biggest contributor to climate change in terms of overall emissions (around 11 per cent), agriculture – and in particular, livestock farming for meat and dairy – is the single most dangerous threat to our planet thanks to the powerful and active nature of the methane gas it creates, the huge amount of resources it takes up, and the wasteful farming methods used.

The Facts About Meat

Here are some facts from some of the most recent, most comprehensive studies, which highlight why the demand for meat is such a huge contributor to climate change:

 To produce 100 g (3½ oz) of beef creates up to 105 kg (231 lb) of greenhouse gases, compared to less than 4 kg (9 lb) to produce 100 g (3½ oz) of tofu.

 Meat production is one of the least efficient forms of farming, taking up 83 per cent of global farmland to produce just 18 per cent of the calories consumed. Research has shown that if we all ditched meat and dairy, we could return 75 per cent of the world's farmland to wilderness, while still having enough food to put an end to global hunger for good.

45

Scientists have now proven that even low-impact meat and dairy products are still worse for the environment than the least sustainable cereal and vegetable production. Not only does meat production use up to 160 times more land than is needed to produce grains (largely because 30 per cent of the world's arable farmland is dedicated to growing feed for livestock rather than for humans), it's also far more water-intensive, and contributes to global acidification.

 To produce 1 lb (453 g) of beef requires over 9,100 litres (2,400 gallons) of water. To produce 1 lb (453 g) of wheat requires 95 litres (25 gallons) of water. This means that if you stopped showering for six months, you'd still not have saved as much water as if you had said no to that single pound of beef.

Even grass-fed beef still has a much higher impact on global warming than any plant-based foods.

 While lamb creates fewer carbon emissions than beef, sheep also provide less edible meat, meaning that pound for pound it's also no friend to the environment.

 Just producing 1 lb (453 g) of pork, one of the most efficient meat types, creates the equivalent carbon footprint of driving a car for 19 km (12 miles).

 A meat-heavy diet creates carbon dioxide emissions of 7.2 kg (15 lb 12 oz) per day, while a vegan diet contributes just 2.9 kg (6 lb 5 oz) per day.

Cutting Meat From Your Diet

 Adopt "meat-free Mondays", or try not eating meat for three days a week. Once you start to omit meat from your meals, and to view vegetables and pulses as the main ingredient rather than a side dish, the realization dawns that meat is not as essential as perhaps we thought. Protein can be obtained from other sources such as pulses, beans, seitan, nutritional yeast, sprouted grains, spelt, hemp, legumes and tofu.

 Grass-eating animals such as cows and sheep are the worst offenders in methane gas production, so eating free-range poultry or pork rather than beef or lamb will have a lesser impact. However, methane is released into the atmosphere with the production of all meat, so limiting your consumption will help, regardless!

If you must eat meat, buy the best-quality meat you can afford and align yourself with meat suppliers who value environmental considerations and animal welfare.

 When in a restaurant, consider the vegetarian option, even if you are not a vegetarian. Experiencing food prepared in different ways can alter your attitudes to meat. Restaurant chefs will have perfected the cooking of all ingredients; see what they do with vegetables and you will be pleasantly surprised!

 Experiment with cooking vegetables and vegan-alternative foods. Most people who dislike vegetables just haven't had them cooked in the right way; try sticky orange and ginger tofu, maple-roasted root vegetables, stir-fried greens with garlic butter or pasta dishes with fried mixed veg, and you'll never go back to plain boiled veg again! And salads should never be boring – spice them up with chopped nuts, dried fruit, seeds, delicious dressings and warm vegetables.

 In dishes where you can barely even taste the meat, such as curries, chilli or mince dishes such as Bolognese or pies, swap the meat for soy mince, lentils, tofu or seitan, plus chopped mixed 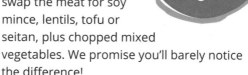 vegetables. We promise you'll barely notice the difference!

 Learn to gradually tip your vegetables-to-meat ratio by slowly changing the proportions of your meals: instead of sausages, bacon and eggs, try sausages, baked beans and fried mushrooms; instead of steak and chips, try a smaller piece of steak, roasted vegetables and salad.

Fish

Fish production is generally considered to have less of an environmental impact than the rearing of land mammals, but it is not without ecological considerations. Fisheries may have a lower impact in terms of energy usage and greenhouse-gas emissions, but we know that extensive fishing has dramatically depleted ocean supplies. Here are the main considerations when buying (and therefore creating demand for) fish:

 As a result of commercial fishing for species commonly eaten by humans, other marine species such as dolphins, sea turtles, sharks and whales are being inadvertently caught (referred to as "bycatch") or tangled up in the nets of trawlers.

Some of our oceans and seas have been overfished to the point that some marine species are close to extinction, causing a dramatic imbalance in the marine food chain. Evolution doesn't work fast enough for the ecosystem in our oceans to catch up with human impacts.

Now fisheries have also been shown to contribute to greenhouse-gas emissions as the build-up of excrement from the fish on the fishery floors decomposes, releasing harmful gases on a scale that was previously unrecognized.

Fishing nets are made of strong plastic that does not break down over time (some say it takes as long as 600 years for a fishing net to decompose) and the nets also create a lethal tangle of plastic in which marine life gets trapped.

 Microplastics and synthetic microfibres that fish consume mean that when we eat fish, we are consuming high levels of these manmade products ourselves. It's also well-documented that certain fish contain dangerously high levels of mercury, so overall we need to consider whether eating fish should even be considered a healthy option at all.

Buying Fish

If you must eat fish, you can reduce your impact on the environment by following these steps:

 Eat sustainably sourced or line-caught fish. As with meat, buy the best you can afford.

 Broaden your taste and try fish that are less commonly offered in supermarkets. This will reduce demand for fish stocks of overfished species. These vary depending on where in the world you are, but the list of most endangered species runs into the double digits and is regularly updated, so check which species you should avoid on a trusted online website.

 Support small, local fisheries. These fishermen make their living from adopting sustainable methods.

 If you must eat tuna, choose skipjack or yellowfin which have been line-caught.

Fish such as carp are herbivores, and are farmed in small ponds. These fish have a lower impact as they are not fed with fishmeal (where fish are caught to feed fish).

For shellfish choose hand-gathered rather than dredged scallops, whelks and cockles. Choose pot-caught crabs and lobsters. These long-established methods are more environmentally sound. The most ecological option when it comes to shellfish may be bivalves – oysters, mussels and clams – whose biological makeup is closest to plant forms. Mussels are grown on ropes in the sea, use up little energy and, as an added bonus, absorb carbon dioxide in their shells.

COFFEE AND TEA

Sadly even things we thought of as innocent pleasures like a good cup of tea or coffee leave an imprint on the environment. Here are the things to look out for:

TEA

In order to seal the tea leaves inside the mesh bag, most big-brand teabags contain polypropylene, a chemical that contributes to plastic pollution. There are biodegradable and compostable teabags available on the market, or you could use loose-leaf tea instead.

COFFEE PODS

The same applies for coffee pods which due to being made of plastic and aluminium take up to 500 years to break down. A former leading executive of a well-known coffee-pod manufacturer

vehemently asserts that the pods are pollutants and has suggested that we, as consumers, reconsider their use, the belief being that the environment should not be sacrificed for convenience. Coffee-pod manufacturers offer collection and recycling programmes, so take advantage of them if you must use coffee pods.

COFFEE BEANS

A more ecological alternative is to buy coffee beans and grind them yourself, as and when you need them.

COFFEE GROUNDS

Used coffee grounds, which are compostable, can be utilized as a pest repellent in the garden. Plants that like an acidic soil will also benefit from a covering of used coffee grounds.

Understanding Genetically Modified Food

A decade or so ago, genetically modified (GM) food received a bad press, with consumers abruptly altering their buying habits to avoid anything that claimed to be GM. But in reality, though to some it still sounds a bit sci-fi, or like our food is being tampered with, GM food has been proven not to cause any ill effect to human life. GM food is simply food where the DNA has been altered to achieve optimum traits, and in that regard humans have been involved in some form of genetic modification for centuries, since monks first cross-bred species of peas to alter their shape and colour. GM food was developed to create bug-resistant, slow-ripening versions of crops, especially crops that were in high demand. What's more, the environmental credentials of GM food are better than first thought: they're produced far more efficiently and on a mass scale, feeding more people with less land. If you add in crop optimization, which promotes the use of less intense farming techniques, all of these factors combined have a favourable impact on the environment. So don't shy away from GM crops; they can feed more people for less, which has got to be a good thing.

Understanding Organic Food

Organic food certification is a complex area. We can deduce that avoiding crops treated with pesticides will be healthier for us, and in turn we know that organically produced crops will reduce the chemical run-off into the water system. However, organic farming means more land is used for less yield, so this method still carries an environmental penalty in terms of efficiency. It also gives people a false sense of security, as despite many believing that an "organic" label, especially on meat, means high welfare standards and therefore less animal cruelty, this is not always true. Look into all the factors behind the production of a given foodstuff and make a reasoned decision for yourself. Do you like the idea of organic, non-GM food because of the lack of pesticides, or do you prefer the idea of more efficient and effective crop growth that can feed more people, thus reducing global hunger. If it worries you, you can always do your own research into individual farms to see whether you agree with their practices and principles. Organic doesn't always mean environmental; we should all be discerning consumers.

PALM OIL

Palm oil is estimated to be present in up to 50 per cent of household products in developed countries – it's in our food, our cleaning products, our fuel and even our make-up – and accounts for around 30 per cent of all vegetable oil production. But what's the problem?

Deforestation

Global demand (60 million tonnes annually) for this cheap oil has driven producers to clear land for more oil palm trees at an alarming and destructive rate. Some estimates put the amount of land being cleared at the equivalent of 300 football pitches every hour. There are currently 27 million hectares (104,000 sq miles) of land, primarily in Borneo and Sumatra, devoted to growing palm oil, and as more land is bulldozed or even burned to make more space for the crop, the land loses all biodiversity and indigenous species lose their habitats. The animal you'll hear most about is the orangutan, and for good reasons: over 90 per cent of their traditional habitat has been lost in the last two decades alone, with data from the government of Indonesia suggesting that over 50,000 orangutans have already died in the last 20 years as a direct result of land clearance for palm oil production. Other species, such as the Sumatran tiger, are also at risk of extinction in years to come if we continue creating more demand for palm oil.

Greenhouse Gases

Indonesia surpassed the USA for greenhouse gas emissions in 2015, and will probably do so again if it continues along its current path. That is due not only to the gases emitted by the burning of the rainforest, but also to the biofuels made primarily with palm oil which have an impact on climate change three times higher than traditional fossil fuels.

Human Cost

And that's to say nothing of the toll on human lives that palm oil production takes. Not only has the industry been linked to horrific human-rights violations including child labour, it also destroys the environment and ecosystem that local people rely on. And the palm oil itself is hardly our friend: the fatty acids it contains have been linked to cancers and damage to our DNA.

So What's The Solution?

Well the first thing is to start reading labels, actively avoiding as many products as you can that contain palm oil.

Luckily, alternatives are emerging every day, with large brands such as Iceland Foods in Europe committing to the removal of all palm oil (as well as plastic packaging from their products over the next few years. Avoiding palm oil will be easiest if you're buying wholefoods and cooking meals from scratch. Swap vegetable oils containing palm oil for soy, rapeseed or sunflower oils for the time being (though do remember to check the labels). Keep an eye out for future developments; scientists are currently looking at ways to develop sustainable alternatives to palm oil.

Packaging

Bananas, avocados, coconuts, nuts… they already have their own strong and hygienic skins, and yet some retailers insist on packing them in plastic. It's not just the obvious culprits – lunch options with unnecessary plastic containers for sauces, or superfluous plastic trays, or plastic bags within boxes are all contributing to this over-packaged consumer landscape. Here are our top tips for escaping the curse of packaging:

 Opt for items packed in paper or cardboard, which will decompose in a relatively short timeframe (especially compared to the plastic alternative).

 Buying canned or tinned foods can be better for the environment than frozen food in non-recyclable plastic bags or overly packaged dry goods, as most areas can effectively recycle steel or aluminium tins without any loss of quality.

Ask retailers whether they have plastic-free options, and, if not, ask that they pass on a request for plastic-free alternatives.

 Buy loose fruit and vegetables, and either pack them in your own cotton vegetable bags or in paper bags.

 Shop at "refilleries" (see p.27) where you can bring in your own reusable plastic or glass containers to stock up on things like rice, oats, pasta, lentils and other grains and legumes.

 Make your own lunches and bring them in to work in reusable plastic containers or glass jars rather than buying overly-packaged sandwiches or salads. It'll also save you loads of money! If you really must buy lunch on the go, look for bakeries or cafes that will sell you a freshly made sandwich on a real plate, rather than one that's wrapped in plastic.

AVOIDING FOOD WASTE

Don't Buy It!

The easiest way to avoid throwing food away is to avoid buying food you aren't going to use in the first place! Plan your meals for the week ahead so you know what ingredients you'll need, and don't buy any extras that will just go to waste.

Buy Only What You Need

If a recipe calls for an ingredient you don't think you'll use again, look for small quantities (usually available at a refillery) or substitute it for another ingredient you already have, to avoid having to throw away a surplus.

Get To Know Your Food

Understanding how foods behave over time is a helpful exercise. For instance, if you know that fish becomes unappealing (and possibly unsafe to eat) after three days,

and that salad leaves can pass their prime within around 48 hours, but potatoes, root vegetables and other sturdy foods can last much longer, you'll know that you need to cook up the fish and serve it with a salad in the first day or two to use everything up, before turning to the vegetables with a longer shelf life.

Best Before

Don't rely on "best before" dates. The "use by" date refers to the date after which food could be considered unsafe, so is best abided by, but "best before" is an optional guideline. A yogurt doesn't become unsafe at the stroke of midnight on the "best before" date, so as long as there's no mould, slimy film, rancid smell or funny texture on the food, and it still looks and smells as you'd expect it to, it's probably fine to use.

Using Up Leftovers

 Think about ways you can use the same ingredients to cook up different meals. For instance, if you are a meat eater and you want to roast a whole chicken, the leftovers could be used in a risotto, a pie or a soup on the following days, so nothing has to be thrown away. You can even use the bones to make a stock.

 Most leftovers can be used for soups, stir-fries, bubble and squeak, chilli, wraps, omelettes and frittatas.

 Soft vegetables like spinach, kale, courgettes, tomatoes, mushrooms and broccoli can be thrown into just about any dish to add flavour and texture.

 Overripe bananas make the best banana bread, or if you chop them and freeze them, you'll have near-instant healthy ice cream at the press of a blender button.

 A glut of ripe tomatoes make the best slow-cooked sauce when baked with crushed garlic and olive oil.

 Turn any past-its-best fruit into a healthy and delicious smoothie.

 Bread that's gone stale (as long as it's not gone mouldy) can be baked to make croutons, turned into breadcrumbs, or used in bread pudding or French onion soup.

 Though people have been put off using leftover rice due to worries about reheating, as long as you store it in the fridge fairly quickly after its initial cooking, it's fine to reuse rice in dishes like egg-fried rice, arancini balls, burger patties, stews and even rice pudding.

PRESERVING FOOD

Preparing and cooking batches of food as soon as ingredients arrive in your home means that precious nutrients are not lost and it also extends their shelf life considerably.

FREEZE THEM

Cook up batches of soup, stews or roast vegetables, then freeze them in individual portions in reusable containers, ready to be cooked up in the future.

ROAST THEM

If you have large quantities of root vegetables that are on the verge of going off, roast them all up and allow to cool, then store in an airtight container in the fridge for up to three more days or in the freezer for up to two weeks.

PRESERVE THEM

Learn how to preserve food. Look up tutorials on salting meats, making preservative acidic dressings, or making chutneys, jams or pickles out of leftover fruit and veg.

FOOD STORAGE TIPS

Spices

Dried spices and herbs are brilliant for cooking from scratch and will convert ordinary foods into something more interesting. But keeping a spice rack of every conceivable spice, on the off chance you might use one, will clog up your kitchen. Instead rely on fresh herbs (you could even grow your own – see p.140), and stick to five or six key spices such as turmeric, ground coriander, paprika, chilli, curry powder and nutmeg to do the job of many.

Mason Jars

Store rice, oats, sugar, flour and other staples in airtight Mason jars; this looks orderly and keeps these foodstuffs fresh.

An Ordered Fridge

Invest in glass fridge storage containers that you will use and reuse. Having an ordered fridge means it's possible to see what food you have, and what you might concoct as a meal, rather than reaching for a ready meal or prepackaged option.

Vegetables

Keeping root vegetables such as potatoes, squash and parsnips in a darkened place will preserve their life. But don't store them with onions, as they both release moisture and gases that cause the other one to spoil more quickly. Store onions separately in a cool, dark, ventilated place.

FOOD COVERINGS

Most households contain a roll of cling film or Saran wrap to cover foodstuffs. As we came to understand more about food hygiene, and concerns loomed large about cross-contamination or leaving food exposed to the air to go off more quickly, this seemed like the perfect hygienic and convenient solution. But at what cost? Every time we throw a non-recyclable piece of plastic wrap in the bin, we risk it ending up in the stomach of a sea creature or tied around the neck of a bird. And there are alternatives, too – it just takes a bit of initiative to change this habit and look into other options.

BEESWAX

Beeswax food covers are fabrics impregnated with natural beeswax, which keep food fresh. They are also reusable, and it's possible to repeatedly clean them, rather than disposing of them.

REUSABLE CONTAINERS

Store food in airtight containers such as jars or plastic containers, instead of wrapping it in plastic.

AVOID ALUMINIUM

Aluminium foil takes a lot of resources to produce. Instead of using foil when grilling and baking, invest in reusable alternatives such as lidded dishes or, if not, use parchment paper. If you must use foil, use a brand which has already been recycled, so the energy needed to produce it is less.

RECYCLING FOIL

Ensure that you recycle any foil you do use if your local recycling facilities allow for it, making sure it is clean, as this will help recycling depots to process it.

TRAVEL

Rethinking how you travel is one of the big ways in which you can improve your carbon footprint (a carbon footprint is the amount of carbon dioxide released into the atmosphere by any single individual's activities). It might not always be possible for everyone, but green driving choices will have a positive cumulative impact. We all know this already, but to reiterate, you do have options:

Walk instead of drive; you'll cut your emissions to zero and enjoy the health benefits, too.

 Cycle instead of drive; you'll cut your emissions to zero and again you'll enjoy the health benefits.

 Car-share; you'll share the emissions with other people, reducing your individual carbon footprints.

 Take the bus, train or tram instead of driving, and you will also cut your emissions drastically; although they typically also use fossil fuel, mass forms of public transport carry tens or even hundreds of people in a single journey, so they greatly diminish your own personal usage.

Using A Car

When running a car, aim to optimize its performance by the following methods so as to achieve the greatest possible fuel economy:

 Check your car's tyre pressure; underinflated tyres can increase fuel consumption by 3 per cent.

 Make sure your car gets a regular service; a well-tuned car performs at an optimum level.

 Slow down; observe the national speed limits in place and drive without abrupt stops and starts. Steady, measured driving is more efficient and uses less fuel.

 Don't idle the engine. If you are going to be stopped for longer than ten seconds, turn off the engine.

Opening a window for air is marginally better than using air conditioning; but both reduce a car's performance, so reconsider long trips in the heat of the day if it's going to be an issue.

 Travel light; the heavier the load, the more fuel is used. Remove roof racks, as these will cause drag and in turn will consume more fuel.

 When and if you are choosing a new car, consider a hybrid or electric model.

 When washing your car, refrain from using strong chemical cleaners which will wash off into the water system. To conserve water, use a bucket rather than a hose (see p.93).

Going On Holiday

We know that flying is not a neutral activity when it comes to the environment. Aeroplanes burn finite fossil fuels, emit greenhouse gases and leave contrails (vapour trails) at high altitude which are thought to affect our climate.

 If you are flying, travel direct rather than taking a cheaper but more complicated route; taking off and landing an aeroplane is what uses up the most fuel.

 Wherever possible, choose airlines that offer ways of offsetting carbon emissions.

 Consider alternatives – could you reach your destination by train instead and turn it into a railway adventure? Or if it's not a long journey, coaches will be a more energy-efficient choice.

Unless you're specifically going on a new, efficient and eco-friendly cruise, cruising may have an even worse impact on the environment than other forms of transport. Apart from the carbon emissions often working out much higher per mile travelled than those for a flight, cruise ships have been criticized for poor waste and water-treatment practices which adversely affect the oceans, as well as the damage they can do to the ports where they call, which are often underprepared to receive the large number of day-trippers disembarking from the ships.

Eco Holidaying

When looking for somewhere to stay, choose places that advocate and employ environmental practices: encouraging recycling, avoiding single-use plastics, following eco-friendly laundry practices, using renewable energy sources, or serving local and seasonal produce in their restaurants. Most hotels, guesthouses and restaurants will make a thing of any eco-friendly credentials they have, or you can look at reviews on sites like TripAdvisor to find out what other visitors made of it. If you want to be sure you're having the kind of holiday Mother Nature herself would enjoy, seek out one of the many eco-friendly, sustainable green lodges, yurts or even igloos for the environmentally conscious traveller that are popping up in many destinations.

. Consider backpacking or walking holidays, staying at local campsites if you want to travel within your own country or region, or look for eco-friendly smaller ships with renewable energy sources if you like the idea of a sailing or boating holiday.

 Just as you would while at home, remember to turn off lights, taps and air-conditioning whenever they're not in use, and try to create as little waste as you can – the locals and the environment will thank you.

 Eating locally in small, independent restaurants is one of the great joys of going on holiday, so I don't need to convince you of their merits. But independent restaurants are also more likely to use local, seasonal food and have more eco-friendly policies, so it's a win-win for you and the planet!

Decant your existing personal products (shampoos, body washes, etc.) into small, reusable pots or bottles, rather than buying single-use travel versions every time.

 Avoid using the mini free toiletries provided by hotels; the average chain hotel will dish out 23,000 mini bottles every year. Instead support hotels that offer larger refillable bottles with dispensers.

SUNTAN LOTION

Look for ethical and ocean-friendly suntan lotions if you're going to be on the beach or going in the sea. Sun creams with oxybenzone are extremely harmful to coral reefs and marine life, and an alarming amount of it washes off our bodies and into the water. High amounts of the chemical have been found on coral reefs, deforming young corals and disrupting their growth, and contributing to coral bleaching, which is irreversible. If we lose our coral reefs, the seas' ecosystems will collapse, with potentially devastating consequences flowing from the subsequent lack of biodiversity and disruption to the food chain. Choose natural alternatives or those certified as reef-friendly, and always use lotion rather than a spray bottle, as the latter ends up spraying the solution onto the sand, from where it washes into the sea. Use aloe vera plant leaf or milk to apply to sunburn.

WATER CONSERVATION

Water is a finite resource and its conservation has become a major environmental concern. The effects of global warming loom large when we see our reservoirs running dry, hosepipe bans and even limitations placed on domestic water usage in periods of drought. But why has this become such an issue?

Only 3 per cent of the world's water is drinkable, with the majority of this currently stored inaccessibly within the polar ice caps. And while the amount of freshwater on earth remains roughly the same through the centuries (thanks to the water cycle's constant recycling), our population is now dramatically bigger than it was even a hundred years ago, meaning resources are **more under strain than they have ever been before**. We are also using far more water nowadays for agriculture and industry, putting even more pressure on this precious resource. If we are to avoid a global crisis and save the world, we need to find ways to effectively manage and conserve our water supplies, and to reduce unnecessary water consumption.

Human beings all need water to survive, but there are ways we can all reduce our water footprint. There are two types of water usage: direct and indirect. Direct is the type we're probably most aware of: it's the water we drink, the water we use to wash our clothes, bodies, dishes and cars, the water that flushes the toilet and runs down the sink every time we turn on a tap. Luckily, direct water usage is very easy to **manage and reduce**. The second type is the water that's used by other people or systems to create the things we use on a daily basis: the water needed to grow food, to grow cotton and other crops for clothes, the water used by factories producing the goods and the clothing we buy, and even the water needed to produce the plastic to pack it all in. This, the more invisible side of our water usage, can be harder to reduce, but there are still steps we can take to tackle it. But let's start with direct water usage.

Reducing Your Direct Water Use

Most of the things on this checklist can be taken up immediately by the vast majority of people and will make an instant reduction to your water footprint:

 Use a water-saving device in the toilet cistern.

 Do not flush the toilet every time; "if it's yellow, let it mellow".

 Ensure taps aren't left running unnecessarily, for instance, while brushing your teeth or washing your hands and face.

 Fix any dripping taps or leaks as soon as possible.

 Take a shower rather than a bath. A shower commonly uses between 30 and 80 litres (6 and 17 gallons), while a bath takes up 150 to 200 litres (33 to 44 gallons).

If you must take a bath, why not make it more earth-friendly and share it with someone you love? And make it extra eco-friendly by using the cold bathwater to water your garden or plants when you're done.

 Take fewer showers. Unless you have a job or a hobby that gets you very dirty or sweaty on a regular basis, you don't need a shower every day. Your skin and hair will thank you for giving them a break.

 If you have to run the tap for any reason, place a bowl underneath it and use the water to water houseplants or your garden.

 Don't throw away cooking water – some recipes call for a fresh pan of water, but in many cases you could easily reuse the same water, or instead you could use it to make up a stock, or again (when cooled) to water houseplants or your garden.

Cut down on meat or cut it out completely (see p.48).

 Use less water by washing up (filling a bowl rather than running the tap) instead of using a dishwasher (unless you have a very efficient and eco-friendly, newer model). If you do use a dishwasher, only run it when it's full.

 Invest in a water filter to store tap water in the fridge; it'll taste better and will stop you having to run the tap to get cold drinking water.

 Add an aerator to taps to improve water flow without using any extra water.

 Install a water butt in your garden and avoid using hosepipes and sprinklers.

 Water plants in the early morning or evening to prevent the water evaporating in the heat of the day.

Reducing Your Indirect Water Use

It is estimated that up to 95 per cent of our individual water footprint comes from the food we eat. As discussed on p.46, all animal products require a huge amount of water to produce, but even non-animal products can be eye-wateringly inefficient when it comes to water use. Chocolate can take almost as much water to produce as beef, while up to 7,500 litres (2,000 gallons) are needed to produce one pound of nuts, depending on the variety, almonds and cashews being the worst culprits. Even olive oil needs around 6,400 litres (1,700 gallons) per pound of oil produced. And of course, the more processing our foodstuffs have to go through before they reach our plate, the more water will be involved in the manufacture, packaging and transport – yet another reason to buy whole, unprocessed foods and make your own delicious meals!

Other manufactured items come with their own water footprint. It takes 11,350 litres (3,000 gallons) of water to make a smartphone; it takes hundreds of gallons of water to grow the cotton used in clothing (around 2,460 litres/650 gallons to make the average T-shirt); and it takes more than twice the amount of water to produce a single plastic water bottle than can be held within it. One way to reduce your involvement in these water-intensive processes is to buy things that are built to last, rather than buying single- or low-use items that you can see will be disposable and need replacing quickly. Buying fewer items, buying recycled items and buying from companies that actively seek to reduce their water usage and carbon footprint will also bring about huge benefits. See p.124 for more on how you can change your shopping habits to save the world.

And, of course, water is used in creating all the electricity we talked about earlier, so all the energy-saving techniques you have already applied for that reason will help reduce your water footprint, too!

THE PLASTIC PROBLEM

Plastic is one of the hot topics you're probably already aware of in relation to the environmental crisis; our plastic usage is out of hand, and society's tolerance of it until the recent step change in attitudes toward it is a cautionary tale of when a good thing can turn bad. A material that was strong, had longevity and reliability was a godsend for modern lifestyles, but now those very characteristics are the same things causing pollution of the environment as the material either decomposes or, mostly, fails to decompose. So we know there's a problem, but it's hard to fully grasp its true extent. So here are some facts that might help put things into perspective and wake us all up to the fact that we need to take drastic action now.

One of the main problems with plastic is that it just doesn't go away. Once it has been created, it won't decompose for **up to a thousand years**; thinner plastics such as in old-style carrier bags may degrade in as little as 10 years, but that's still 10 years where it may pass through the stomachs, and claim the lives, of hundreds of animals, break into smaller pieces that end up in the human food chain, or simply rot away in landfill, creating methane and hydrogen that is released into the atmosphere as it degrades. And **only 9 per cent of all plastic waste ever created has been recycled**.

Single-use, non-biodegradable plastics are the worst offenders, but it is estimated that around 10 per cent of all waste worldwide is plastic of some sort. Every year over one million tonnes of plastic end up in UK landfill, and in the US the figure is a whopping **28.9 million tonnes**. Even plastics we can barely see and are often oblivious to, such as tiny fragments that erode from our car tyres every time we drive, add up to a horrifying amount of plastic waste that continues to grow. The amount of plastic entering landfill worldwide is **enough to stretch around the earth four times**, and around eight million metric tonnes of plastic ends up in the ocean every year. In 2016 around 335 million tonnes of plastic were produced worldwide; equivalent to **the weight of two million blue whales**. Even with recycling, more packaging is being produced than we can hope to recycle.

Manufacturing plastic uses up 8 per cent of the world's oil production every year, so plastics are intrinsically linked to our use of fossil fuels and cannot be considered a sustainable material.

If these facts don't shock you, perhaps we can try the tugging-at-your-heartstrings approach: manmade litter in the ocean is responsible for **the deaths of around 100,000 marine mammals and one million sea birds** every single year.

And it's not just the environment that can be harmed by plastic. Plastic is a processed combination of chemicals, with some plastics containing toxic or carcinogenic (cancer-causing) chemical compounds. Although  plastic is slow to biodegrade, exposure to the sun and air can cause some plastics to degrade slightly, **leaching hazardous substances into the earth or water around it**. If humans come into contact with these substances – for example, by taking a drink from a plastic bottle that's been sitting in the sun, by drinking water that's been contaminated by plastic waste or by eating marine animals or seafood that have plastic substances in their stomachs – they could be exposed to the chemicals.

But there is hope. Successfully tackling overuse of plastic in our everyday lives can be boiled down to the three main recycling principles: reduce, reuse and recycle. Here are ways you can make a difference and make sure you contribute as little plastic waste as possible to this ever-growing problem.

Avoiding Single-Use Plastics

We must come to understand that something which has a momentary use to a human, and is then discarded, remains in the ecosystem for hundreds of years, immune to decomposition. Here are some quick and easy ways to cut down your dependency on single-use plastics:

 Carry a reusable bottle for water instead of buying bottled water.

 Carry a reusable insulated cup for takeaway hot drinks, or a thermos flask to make and transport your own homemade versions. In one year alone, over 6.5 million trees are cut down, four billion gallons of water are used and 253 million pounds of waste are created to make the 16 billion paper cups used by US consumers for coffee alone.

Keep a reusable cotton, hessian or straw bag for carrying anything you buy. Refuse plastic or paper bags in shops.

 Carry a metal straw and refuse plastic straws. Or when you have a drink, consider whether you actually need a straw. Surely sipping a drink is good enough?

 Carry reusable cutlery – a knife, fork and spoon – so that you can eat when not at home and do not need to use plastic, disposable ones. If bought meals come with plastic cutlery, make a point of refusing it and requesting proper cutlery.

 Plastic drinking straws are so lightweight that they often defy recycling machines, and copious numbers have been washed into our oceans and are mistaken by marine life for food or, worse, become lodged in an animal's body. Request paper straws or go without.

Avoid plastic six pack rings used to keep drinks cans together, as these can ensnare wildlife. Some brands are starting to replace these with biodegradable, natural alternatives, so opt for those instead if you can. If you do acquire any plastic ones, cut them up before putting them in the bin.

 Avoid buying ready meals that come in plastic trays (often with non-recyclable plastic film over the top).

 Buy refillable ink or toner cartridges for office equipment or look into places that recycle single-use plastic cartridges.

 Take your own reusable containers to collect food from your favourite takeaway. If they say they don't offer this as an option and they don't offer a sustainable alternative, take your business elsewhere.

Buy butter in blocks wrapped in paper rather than in tubs.

Microbeads

Microbeads – tiny pieces of plastic added to cosmetic products such as facewash, toothpaste and abrasive cleaners – were deliberately designed to wash down the drain. The result is that sewerage systems cannot capture them, which means routinely they are flushed through the system into the seas and oceans. Although in some countries bans are in place on the production of microbeads, they can still be found and are, of course, a legacy problem. A single plastic particle absorbs up to one million times more toxic chemicals than the water around it, so although small, these particles can have a potent effect on the environment. Avoid their use completely.

REUSING PLASTICS

Reuse plastic items you already own:

PLASTIC BAGS

If they're of the stronger type, put them in your car or bike basket ready for shopping trips. If not, use them for bin liners, take them to a specialist recycling point (often found at supermarkets) or use them for crafting; there are plenty of ideas online, from weaving them into baskets to making them into jewellery, bird feeders, art pieces or even rugs. Or turn them into an ecobrick (see p.106).

FOOD BAGS

Instead of normal, wasteful bin bags, use plastic bags previously deployed to package foods such as cereals or large packets of crisps.

PLASTIC BOTTLES

Plastic bottles can be cut up and used in crafts or turned into pots (just cut off the top), storage containers, herb planters or even homemade watering cans or watering devices for your plants.

MAIL BAGS

Reuse plastic mail bags where possible.

Ecobricks

Ecobricks are a way of dealing with single-use plastic. Stuff any small pieces of plastic you have lying around tightly into a litre-sized plastic bottle until it forms a hard, dense block. You'll be surprised at how much plastic you can keep squashing in! The "brick" can then be used as a crude building material as an alternative to more conventional building materials, especially in developing countries. There is plenty of advice online as to how to create an ecobrick, along with important safety information you should observe if trying this out and what to do with your brick when it's filled to the brim.

NURDLE-HUNTING

Virtually all plastics we use started life as a nurdle, a lentil-sized piece of pre-production, high-density plastic that forms the building block of bags, bottles and just about any plastic item you can think of. These cute-sounding little items are starting to become a big problem. Used globally, they are transported around the world on container ships by the tonne. Billions of them make their way into the ocean annually after accidental spills on factory floors, in transportation to ships and from containers lost from ships. They are found on 73 per cent of UK beaches, and a study in Orange County, USA found them to be the most common beach contaminant. They do not decompose, but simply break into smaller pieces, and are often eaten by marine wildlife with damaging effects to the ingesting animals and to the foodchain as a whole, at the end of which is ourselves.

Many companies are signing up to initiatives that promote sensible nurdle-handling practices to try to curtail this source of pollution, but in the meantime if you want to take action, you can try lobbying plastic-producing companies to take more responsibility for their actions, or attend a beach clean near you to hunt for these tiny but hugely damaging little objects.

AVOIDING PACKAGING

So we're already avoiding items that are made with plastic, but what about perfectly natural or eco-friendly items – books, furniture, technology, clothing – that, especially when bought online, are delivered to you wrapped in swathes of plastic packaging?

Online Shopping

If you're ordering items online, order multiple items at once to reduce separate packaging.

Food Shopping

If you're doing a food shop online, look to see if the company offer a "pack without plastic bags" option; they'll often bring your goods into your kitchen in trays for you to unpack before they take away the trays.

Switch To Cardboard

Choose cardboard or paper packaging, although be aware that even these materials have a footprint; they are made from felled trees and are heavier, leading to more carbon emissions in transportation.

Large Goods

If you are having large items such as furniture or white goods delivered, ensure packaging is taken away at the point of delivery, to be reused or recycled.

Packing

If you're packing an item to be moved, sent somewhere or stored, the best packing material is your own reusable kind – old newspapers, bubble wrap, popped popcorn or old linen or fabrics – or none.

Stop! Before You Throw...

So many products contain plastics and synthetics, from children's toys to lipsticks to garden tools, and in our journey to a greener lifestyle it can be tempting to want to start afresh with natural alternatives made with planet-friendly materials such as wood, wool or linens. But we create even more waste as we dispose of the old items, especially if they haven't reached the end of their useful lifespan.

Even natural materials cause environmental disruption in their manufacture and production, and there is, we must accept, the practice of "greenwashing" among retailers and advertisers, whereby a product that is made to look green and environmentally sound, on closer inspection is found not to be. So don't rush to chuck out all your existing plastic items to be replaced by green alternatives all at once; only get rid of things when they've outlived their usefulness, and then look at options such as donating, recycling or reusing them, rather than putting them in the bin.

PACKAGING: YOU HAVE A VOICE

Who Are You Buying From?

Consider which retailer you buy from;
align with and buy from those who publish
strong sustainability credentials – those who
practice what they preach.

No-Plastic Options

Request a low- or no-plastic packaging
option when you order. Use and champion
companies who agree to accept the return
of their own packaging to be reused.

Ask Questions

Ask companies if they routinely have or are
able to provide a plastic-free delivery option.
Question why larger companies insist
on sending boxes within boxes. Call out
brands and companies who use senseless
excess packaging.

111

Report Back

If you find excessive packaging is used, flag this up to the retailer or brand, expressing your disappointment. Publicize it.

Celebrate The Good Guys

Conversely, applaud and positively publicize retailers and brands who manage the packaging problem innovatively, using more sustainable packaging options such as wadding, 100 per cent recycled plastic, 100 per cent recyclable plastic and shredded paper.

PAPER

Though this may feel like a topic we're all well versed in nowadays, and most people and companies have embraced the idea of recycling paper and buying recycled paper products, it is still a considerable issue affecting our planet. So what's the problem with paper?

First, although most pulp and paper mills use renewable energy and are now fully embracing recycling and much better practices than in years gone by, it's still an incredibly water-intensive industry; in fact, **it uses more water to manufacture one tonne of paper than for the same weight of any other product**. The paper and pulp industry is also energy-intensive, being the fifth-largest consumer of energy in the world. Paper production accounts for **4 per cent of global energy use**. More energy is also used when "deinking" paper products to be recycled.

Deforestation is still an issue for any paper production that isn't sustainable, and even when it is, plantation forests can have their own negative effects on the environment: the ecological effect of such large areas of single crops – creating monocultures – can **be devastating to indigenous species**.

There are also issues arising from the water pollution a paper mill generates, the pulping processes, chemicals used in manufacturing processes and the greenhouse gases released by the industry (though these are at least far smaller than other major industries). **So what can we do?**

Cut Down Your Paper Consumption

 Switch to digital versions of magazines and newspapers.

 Unsubscribe from companies who send you catalogues or junk mail.

 Switch to paperless banking, where you can view all your bank statements and details online, rather than receiving continuous post from them that you know you're not even going to look at.

 Switch to ebooks, borrow books from libraries or friends, and buy second-hand or at least pass on your books (including this one!) when you've finished reading them.

 Embrace e-tickets for flight or event/theatre tickets and set up your smartphone so you are able to store and view documents online.

Digitize receipts rather than taking a paper receipt that will in all likelihood be disposed of. Instead request emailed receipts or no receipt at all when you pay for something – most of the time you either don't need a receipt anyway or the record on your online banking will suffice.

 Where possible, ask for digital versions of any documents – work documents, spreadsheets and other paperwork (even contracts and legal documents) can nearly all be viewed just as well on screen rather than as a printed-out version.

 Avoid printing anything unless you absolutely need to. If you must print, print both sides of the paper and use black and white rather than coloured ink.

Refuse junk mail; sometimes this is as simple as putting a "no junk mail" sticker on your letterbox, but alternatively you could use a mail preference service for your address. This process removes your address where it is registered and ceases unsolicited mail for any members of your household. Similarly, you can register previous occupants of the home you live in, if you receive junk mail for them, too.

 Return junk mail to the sender, letting them know that their unsolicited mail is unwelcome.

 Avoid using paper towels in public toilets by carrying your own small face-cloth-sized towel in your bag.

 Make sure you always recycle any paper that is no longer needed.

Sustainable Paper

Though we can all do our best to cut down on our paper consumption, and cut out unnecessary paper usage completely, there will inevitably be times when we do need something on paper. At those moments we could do the least environmental damage by opting for recycled paper products or buying paper that is regulated and certified by an approved sustainable forest management and legal logging authority, such as the FSC (Forest Stewardship Council) or PEFC (Programme for the Endorsement of Forest Certification) or similar. You could also source paper that is chlorine-free (normally labelled "TCF paper"), which helps alleviate the chemical water pollution some paper mills create.

RECYCLING

Tackling global warming isn't just about reducing the amount of energy, water, plastic and paper we use; it's also about directing your waste to the best place possible to alleviate some of the environmental burden felt by our rapid consumption of stuff. There comes a time when we have to question whether it is sustainable to continue sourcing whatever we want whenever we want it, without having a solution for the waste that is being created by this appetite for more and more consumption.

The first step is to become more adept at curating our homes, of thinking about what we need, what is useful and what simply fills a void. We can aim to avoid duplication or triplication of possessions. We can look to nature instead of synthetics and manmade items which don't biodegrade. Essentially, we should **stop buying things altogether that we will only want to dispose of soon after**. We should aim to reach a point where all disposable items – paper plates, plastic cups, cleaning wipes, paper napkins – are out of the question, and we are not buying things just for the sake of filling space.

Second, we should teach ourselves to understand what can and can't be recycled, and how to make sure it gets to the right place for that to happen. If left in landfill, **a tin can may take 50 years to decompose and a plastic**

bottle a horrifying 450 years. The decomposition of glass is undetermined; we can assume it will last, in some capacity, forever.

And third, we need to make sure that we **send as little to landfill or down the drain as possible.** The only thing that should be flushed down the toilet is bodily waste and toilet paper (cotton-wool buds, face wipes, tampon applicators, etc. should all go in the bin) to alleviate harmful ocean litter.

Recycling Rules

It is a fact that many of the principles that govern what and how much we recycle are set locally. This can mean there are disparities between different regions. Take the time to understand and to utilize the waste management that applies to you locally. Find out how your waste recycling is handled, where it ends up, what is included and so on: you may be surprised to find that your local council accepts products you hadn't thought of as recyclable.

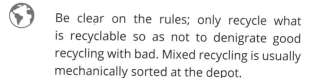 Be clear on the rules; only recycle what is recyclable so as not to denigrate good recycling with bad. Mixed recycling is usually mechanically sorted at the depot.

If your locality doesn't recycle a particular material as a matter of course, find out where these items can be recycled. This may be a frustrating process but it will be worth it to improve your recycling capability.

Keep your recycling dry; wet paper and cardboard clogs up the sorting machines.

Rinse items before you put them in the recycling: food sitting in bins can attract rodents and flies, grow mould and render a batch of otherwise good recycling unusable. But don't waste fresh water on washing them until they sparkle: most recycling depots will burn off any food waste and carry out their own washing processes.

 Electrical appliances can be recycled if they are taken to a designated recycling place. Toasters, microwaves, televisions, DVDs, electric toothbrushes, hairdryers, fridges, power tools and so on can all be recycled.

 Hazardous materials such as antifreeze or acid can also be appropriately handled at a recycling depot. Never pour unused chemicals down the drain!

 Finally, make it easy on yourself! Have a small, neat bin or set of bins to store your waste and recyclables: a smaller bin makes it easier to keep track of the amount of waste you're creating every week and will help you be aware of what you're putting in which bin.

SHOPPING

If we all rethought our shopping habits and considered need over desire, we could change, and save, the world.

Shop Less

Before buying anything, regardless of its eco-friendly credentials, think about it in one, five and ten years' time. Will you still own it? Will it still be something you enjoy? If you can imagine discarding it in the relatively short term, ask yourself if you must have it or whether the world would be better off if you didn't buy it at all. We often believe we need certain items because of modern etiquette or the lure of the advertising industry, but perhaps we just don't.

Question What You "Need"

Do you really need different types of glass for various drinks? Do you need multiple types of plate, bowl and cutlery? Do you need that new outfit, or do you have a perfectly full wardrobe already? Does your pet need a new, custom-made dog bed or can you just add a blanket to its old one to make it more comfortable? If you strongly desire something, try waiting a week before you buy it. If after that amount of time has elapsed you still desire the item, then go ahead. But if the feeling has waned, it's a sign that you were just consuming without real intention.

Reuse And Upcycle

If you "need" a new item – of clothing, furniture, etc. – think first whether you might already own something that would do the trick. With a little love and attention, old items can be given a second lease of life. Try restoring or upcycling furniture made of real wood, rather than buying a new flat-packed piece of "instant" furniture.

Shop Better

Try only buying what you want from a second-hand source. Attend car boot sales and vintage markets, buy from charity shops, thrift shops and antiques shops, or look online at second-hand items for sale. Buying something new creates more demand for manufacturers to build more products, but the chances are that someone who already has an item that would do the job for you doesn't want it anymore and is looking to sell.

Only Buy Things You Actually Want

Avoid taking freebies or two-for-one offers. If you didn't choose it and don't know its eco-credentials, don't take it! Slow down when making purchases. While exciting, the magic of accumulation can get lost when acting in haste. Acquiring objects slowly and with consideration will in the long run be more sustainable. Mistakes will seldom be made when you've longed for something for months, saved up and finally bought it. If you don't love it, don't buy it! If you often find yourself impulse-buying things online or on shopping trips, try restricting your access to retailers. Don't go shopping unless there's something you need, and if you do go shopping, stick to shops that stock sustainable products or have great eco-friendly credentials.

CLOTHES

Clothing is essential for warmth, protection and other practical uses, not to mention that it's socially unacceptable to do without it in most places around the world. But we need to start paying closer attention to our clothing choices. Our appetite for new clothes has expanded exponentially in recent years, along with the emergence of internet shopping, to create "fast fashion", which we now understand has some of the most dire environmental effects. Fast fashion is defined as the production and retail of cheap, fashion-led clothes, made efficiently and consumed in mass quantities. Many of the negative effects of fast fashion can be attributed to the reliance on low-quality manmade fabrics that feature a high level of synthetics. These are released during the wear-and-wash cycle into our water supply. Production methods for certain textiles are also incredibly wasteful as well as harmful to local ecosystems. Mass-produced, poorly made clothes are not even fit for upcycling and cannot be resold, so more often than not they end up in landfill.

A wider implication is that, to keep down the price to consumers, fast fashion is produced in underdeveloped nations using cheap labour. We pretend not to notice that our affordable clothes often mean poor working conditions for those creating them in less privileged parts of the world.

Textile Production

Production and manufacturing of all fabrics have an impact, with cotton being the worst offender when it comes to water use, though linen and wool are not far behind. Synthetic textiles use less water but place a strain on other natural resources used in their production, such as crude oil, which of course emits greenhouse gases. Neither option is environmentally sound, so the best thing to do is to buy good-quality clothing that will last for years without having to be thrown away or replaced. We should therefore ask ourselves before we buy anything: if we were to fast-forward 20 years, would the item of clothing we are holding right now still be doing its job or would it have been discarded long before then?

Manmade Textiles

The development of manmade textiles has meant that polyester, viscose and vinyl have come to the forefront of fashion and home interiors. The development of technical, "wicking" fabrics for sport and leisure has heralded an alternative to traditional natural fibres such as cotton, linen, silk and wool. Our use of manmade fabrics in our homes and in our clothes has grown exponentially, and their ease of use and relative cheapness has meant that until recently we haven't questioned their side effects. In relation to fabrics, it's not only the way in which they might decompose over time, but also the care of them, through washing them in washing machines, that is concerning for the planet. The release of microfibres into the water system from domestic and industrial settings has far-reaching effects for marine life.

Natural Textiles

The use of natural textiles is also not without environmental impact. Approximately half of all textiles created are made of cotton. Cotton production techniques over the past century have evolved to favour the use of pesticides and other chemicals to strengthen cotton crops. Dyes used in fabric production also pollute. These chemicals are absorbed by the soil, from where they run off into the water system. Water is a heavily used component of cotton manufacturing, and we know that it takes more than 20,000 litres (5,280 gallons) of water to produce just 1 kg (2.2 lb) of cotton. To give perspective to this figure, this is roughly enough fabric to create a single T-shirt and a pair of jeans. Not only is this putting a strain on the world's water resources in general, it can also have devastating consequences on the local environment. Buying and using organic cotton can help ensure the cotton has been grown in a more sustainable manner and is one small step we can take toward fixing the problem.

Choosing Clothes

So what can we do? Here are some places to start:

 Try alternative fabrics! Advances have been made with new fibre types such as bamboo, hemp and nettle, and these fabrics perform well compared to the more traditional textiles.

 Choose clothes that fit and suit you! Don't buy (and ultimately discard) clothes that you might wear only once or might soon go off.

 Ask yourself: will I wear this repeatedly, do I need it, and does it complement what I have already?

 Research what you are buying and invest in higher-quality clothes, rather than opting for a cheap, quick fix. Buy only from fashion retailers who conduct their business in an ethical, sustainable and eco-friendly manner. This can take some research and may mean sourcing clothes in a slower and more deliberate way, rather than making impulse purchases.

 Support smaller artisan producers who favour handmade textiles and features. This will support communities in developing countries instead of exploiting them. Champion brands who accept their products back for repair if damaged, and who are willing to recycle if products are returned to them after years of use. This type of cradle-to-grave sustainability shows how it is possible to produce fashion with a conscience.

 Favour the "make do and mend" mentality by reworking existing clothes and fabrics into new ones or fixing wear and tear. This form of upcycling means repairing or enhancing

134

existing clothes for your personal use. Teach yourself a few basic sewing techniques and invest in a basic sewing kit so you can quickly repair any small holes or replace missing buttons.

 Look for vintage finds! The assumption with vintage clothes is that they were made at a time when production ethics were founded on craftmanship and quality, and that, being made of natural fibres, they are sometimes in a "virgin" state, that is, untouched by modern chemicals, dyes and solvents. They are often made of higher-quality fabrics than modern clothes, while small problems like broken zips or fasteners can be easily replaced. If the item already exists, it beats creating more demand for new products!

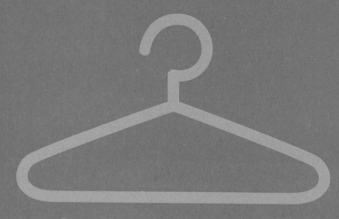

A CAPSULE WARDROBE

In an effort to curb the consumerism that we see in fast fashion, one approach is to consider devising a capsule wardrobe. This premise, which has gained momentum as a movement in recent years, works on the basis that each individual owns a set and limited number of items of clothing to cover every season, rejecting the need to slavishly follow every fashion or trend. Capsule wardrobes contain items that are high-quality, simple, versatile and long-lasting, all of which could be ethically and environmentally sourced. Not only can capsule wardrobes be liberating to the wearer, they have obvious planet-friendly benefits.

CHOOSING A CAPSULE WARDROBE

Limit It

Limit the capsule wardrobe in number (between 30 and 50 items, including shoes and accessories) and only wear those items.

Choose Wisely

Choose clothes wisely and with intention; do not purchase clothes you won't cherish.

Colour Palette

Settle on a cohesive colour palette that is interchangeable and complementary.

One In, One Out

Establish a one-in, one-out approach to buying clothes; only purchase an item if its predecessor is worn out, and make sure you upcycle, donate or responsibly dispose of the old item.

Change Your Attitude

By limiting the number of clothes you buy, the premise is that what you do choose will be the best quality you can afford. This will alter your relationship to buying clothes from buying haphazardly (fast fashion) to buying deliberately and with conscious intention.

IN THE GARDEN

Growing Your Own

If you have access to a garden, consider how you use that space. In urban locations, there are still options for growing window boxes of herbs and salad leaves. But perhaps you have enough land for a vegetable patch. Growing your own food has more than one benefit: plants absorb CO_2 from the atmosphere and increase biodiversity, and there is also the environmental boon of avoiding buying pre-prepared, packaged food, as well as the psychological one of eating things you have grown yourself. By growing your own fruit, vegetables and herbs you can also guarantee that they are both organic and come without the financial and environmental costs of transportation: what you produce can go straight from patch to plate. Those who don't have access to their own garden can look to use community gardens and allotments. Replacing just 20 per cent of the food you eat with produce from a home-grown source will reduce your carbon footprint by nearly 32 kg (70 lb) of CO_2 per year.

A GREEN GARDEN

HAVE SOME PRINCIPLES

Apply the same principles to your garden as you would to your household: buy in bulk, avoid plastics, select plants and tools with quality and not quantity in mind. Reduce waste and try to avoid harmful chemicals.

ECO MATERIALS

Choose eco materials in your garden, sourced locally (reducing the carbon footprint of transportation), and eliminate chemicals and pesticides which affect the soil composition and enter the water system.

AU NATUREL

Employ traditional, natural methods to deal with garden pests, such as egg shells to deter slugs. Peppermint, clove and rosemary essential oils are unpalatable to garden pests.

LET THE WATER IN

Choose permeable materials in your garden, especially in areas of paving and patio. This lessens water run-off and instead allows water to soak naturally into the earth. Use stone and other materials which are local to you.

HEDGEHOG-FRIENDLY

Ensure the perimeter of your garden fencing has hedgehog holes through which hedgehogs can roam.

FEED THE BIRDS

Hang a bird feeder. This helps those avian species who need support, but also brings biodiversity to your garden. Eco bird feeders are specially designed to utilize materials which are environmentally sound.

SAVE WATER

Buy or make a rainwater storage system – a large container, barrel or water butt that collects rainwater, which you can then use to wash your car, water your plants or even to flush toilets.

GROWING PLANTS AND TREES

Stay Native

Select plants that are native. Attempting to grow plants from other regions and countries will require more care, while non-native plants may wipe out native species, potentially unsettling the ecology of your garden and even the local area.

Succulents

Grow succulents. They require significantly less fertilizer, less grooming, less pruning, less maintenance and, generally, less water than other kinds of plant.

Offset Emissions

Planting trees is one way to offset carbon emissions. Select trees with large leaves and broad crowns, which are the most efficient at absorbing carbon and enabling photosynthesis. Trees that are native to your local climate grow quickly, so they will start to make a difference sooner and will have a longer life expectancy.

Garden Recycling

Use recycled materials to grow plants. You can plant seeds in cardboard toilet rolls, plant vegetables such as potatoes in old tyres and cut off bottoms from plastic pots and bottles to germinate seeds or grow herbs.

Get Into Composting

Half of what the average household sends to landfill – amalgamated waste, rather than that which is sorted for recycling – is compostable material, mainly from the kitchen, although a much smaller proportion is gardening waste. In landfill, food scraps do not compost down, as this process requires air. Instead they rot anaerobically, giving off methane gas – one of the most potent greenhouse gases – which traps heat in the atmosphere, leading to global warming and associated climate change.

 If you don't have a garden, find or start a "compost collective", whereby multi-dwelling buildings share composting activity to promote the practice. There are also organizations that accept donated compostable waste and will do the job for you.

Aerate your compost once a week by turning the contents over with a garden fork or an aeration tool.

 You can give your compost a boost by adding a compost activator that speeds up the process.

 You can buy worms or otherwise encourage them into your compost heap to help speed up the process, or you could invest in a wormery, which is different to a composter but helps get rid of kitchen waste in an environmentally friendly way. Look online for more tips.

 If you have a garden, put your food and garden waste in a compost bin or make your own composter. Tutorials for DIY options abound online.

What To Put In Your Compost

 For kitchen waste, composting needn't be a complex process. Take food scraps, peel, leftovers, teabags, coffee grounds and put them aside in a receptacle.

 By separating out food waste, overall household wastage decreases, less is sent to landfill, and your bin smells all the better and requires less frequent emptying.

 If the aroma of leftover food is troublesome, keep food scraps in the freezer and empty out once a week for composting.

 Put in fallen leaves, plant and grass cuttings, as long as they don't have diseases, but avoid putting in weeds.

 Never put any meat, dairy or excrement in your compost heap, as these will lead to unwanted pests and smells.

 Fabric that is 100 per cent cotton can be compostable; remove all elastic, labels and adornments, cut into thin strips or squares and put them in a compost bin. Synthetic fibres do not compost, but cotton rags will decompose in less than six months.

HENS AND BEES

If you're not against the idea of keeping animals or using their produce, and you can offer them a happy and safe place to live, there are benefits to keeping hens or bees in your garden.

BEAUTIFUL BEES

The honeybee is becoming an endangered species. Consider keeping a hive for honey and to support local pollination; as a happy side effect, your vegetable garden yields will be boosted, too. Beeswax is a side product that can be utilized to make candles, lip balms, soaps and polishes, while bee pollen, collected by local bees, is thought to be a natural remedy for allergies and other ailments. Propolis or bee glue also has medicinal benefits and can be harvested to treat pain and ailments requiring antibacterial attention.

HAPPY HENS

Consider keeping hens for their eggs. Hens eat kitchen trimmings and garden cuttings, therefore reducing the waste from your home. By sourcing eggs from your own home, you will reduce the transport impact of buying them from a shop. Give surplus eggs to neighbours and friends so as to reduce their carbon footprint too. Hens can reduce pests in a garden, eat fallen fruits and offer a pleasant spectacle to look at, as well as being affectionate pets – yes, really! Their manure can also be added to compost to form a highly nutritious fertilizer for your plants.

CELEBRATIONS

The futility of using disposable items becomes clear when we consider celebrations such as Christmas, Halloween, summer picnics and birthday parties. As these events approach, we habitually arm ourselves with themed, disposable decorations, gifts, food and cards, all in the name of convenience and tradition. Christmastime is an especially pertinent example, when it sometimes seems that the lure of advertising and retail conspires to promote consumerism and acquisitiveness far more aggressively than at any other time of the year. But there are still ways to celebrate these occasions with our loved ones without drastically increasing our carbon footprint or losing our green credentials.

Avoid Disposables When Celebrating

 Avoid paper plates, cups, placemats and cutlery. Use standard alternatives and just commit to doing a bit more washing up at the end.

 Use linen or cotton napkins rather than disposable ones.

 Avoid single-use, disposable place settings, table decorations, balloons, glitter sprinkles and so on.

 Do not use Chinese lanterns. They not only pose a fire risk, but the leftover metal parts can also injure wildlife and livestock.

 Decorate your home with items from nature. Invest in bulbs that will grow into hyacinths and amaryllis in spring. Paint hens' eggs at Easter. Grow flowers in your garden to cut and display in the summer months.

Adorn your home with gourds, squashes and pumpkins in autumn. Use eucalyptus, mistletoe, holly and ivy at Christmas. Invest in art made from recycled materials, and seek out artists and designers who work with materials that have been discarded by others.

GREEN GIFTS

We all love to give gifts, as giving makes us feel good. However, consumerism and advertising combined have created a powerful force that is often damaging to the environment. Maybe it's time to rethink the point of giving. Do we need more physical things or would the gift of an experience be better? There are countless ideas for experiential gifts on the market, but why not create a simple homemade voucher inviting someone to spend time with you doing something they love: a perfect, thoughtful gift that involves no unnecessary wrapping paper.

Rethink the "gift pack" mentality: preselected and prepackaged sets containing extraneous packaging that often amounts to more than the products themselves. Smaller product sizes entail inefficiency. Why buy small versions of multiple products when the chances are you only need one?

Gift Ideas

The best gifts are those which have a timeless appeal on account of their simplicity, beauty, utility or longevity. Focus on giving gifts that are edible, reusable or sustainable. In short, give gifts you'd like to receive yourself.

Examples of green gifts include:

Sewing kit

Block of quality milled soap

Seeds to plant

Linen napkins

Yoghurt-making kit

Cider or beer-making kit

Apple press

This book about saving the planet!

Home-grown flowers or vegetables

High-quality and sustainably produced
olive oil, wine and honey

Anything homemade or upcycled

Sponsorship of a well, toilet or
water-treatment facility for a family or
community in a developing country

**Sponsorship of a child, school
or community project in a
developing country**

WRAPPING PAPER AND CARD GIVING

If you still want to give a gift in the form of an object, make sure you take care with its presentation.

WRAP IN ECO-STYLE

Most wrapping paper is non-recyclable. Seek out recycled and recyclable paper, if using any at all, or use brown paper that you can spruce up with stamps or hand-drawn decorations, or even newspaper (just try to avoid a page with a horrible headline on it!). Ribbons, tags and other flourishes are invariably made of plastic-coated materials, so look for muslin cloth or fabric alternatives that can be reused next year.

DITCH THE CARDS

Giving cards is a long-held and established tradition, but one that is not very planet-friendly. Many cards are the equivalent of single-use plastics; although a small number have a lovely sentiment you will want to treasure for years, many do not and only adorn our homes for a short time before being discarded. They're rarely recyclable, too – especially those with glitter or shiny surfaces on the front. Reconsider this tradition. Would a phone call or an e-message work just as well? Or a letter on recycled paper?

REUSING CARDS

Reuse old Christmas and birthday cards by cutting out nice images from the front and using them as gift tags. You could even use the backs or any blank space for writing shopping lists or notes, if you need to write something down.

ACTIVISM

Don't worry, the burden of saving the world doesn't rest solely on your shoulders! There are all sorts of individuals, groups and initiatives out there already working hard to reduce both the creation and consumption of plastic, to reduce carbon emissions and paper and water waste, to raise awareness of the issue of climate change and to bring it to the attention of the media and the government. Join in with other like-minded people and lend your voice to their cause, because we're all in this together!

Some may not consider their individual actions to be important, believing the hard work is all down to governments and corporations. Some cannot fathom how efforts made on a personal level can in any way help the planet on which we live.

But leaving it to government institutions, corporations and those in positions of power to set the tone by adding the green agenda to their list of priorities is starting to feel like a risky strategy; given the speed with which environmental degradation has taken place in the last decade, it's clear that **urgent action is key**. Waiting for policymakers might mean any meaningful change comes far too late.

The beauty of activism in this area is that **there are things we can do personally to affect change**; appreciating that fact is empowering and even inspiring. The aim should be to help others understand what they also can do, to foster sensible behaviours and to make measured choices about what we do, buy, consume and acquire.

Get Involved!

 Get involved in any initiatives springing up in your local area: beach cleans if you live by the coast and other litter-collection exercises inland.

 Strong messages need to be sent by consumers to brands to change the way they manufacture, package and market their produce. We as consumers can play a crucial role in affecting change, by actively ceasing to buy products that aren't environmentally friendly and by writing to retailers that sell these products to urge them to change their ways.

 Volunteer for charities which support the environmental agenda, aligning yourself with their work and offering support by donating your money, time or ideas. Participate in sponsored events, campaigning and raising awareness for your chosen charity. Use all channels open to you to bring about change in the home, in your place of work and in the public sphere.

Lobby your local governing body to take action on any (or all) of the issues raised in this book. Many effective campaigns start at local level, where the attention of local politicians is easier to attract. It's much easier to gain wider traction on a particular issue when you already have people in power on your side. Good issues to tackle include reducing litter and combatting waste in your local area.

 Take responsibility for this issue and do what needs to be done! It can be easy to offset the pressure to take action onto a charity by donating money or surplus possessions and hoping for the best. Take ownership of what happens within your own life and make positive changes to do better than the status quo.

 Follow the work of others you admire. Mimic their actions, be hungry for suggestions, going above and beyond them where you can!

Environmental Social Media

One of the most potent forms of environmental activism is the use of social-media platforms. Never before has there been such a direct route to make industries and corporations aware of their environmental practice. Social-media sites such as Twitter and Instagram enable ordinary consumers to reflect their views outward and to start public discussions about practices or products that deserve attention, either to highlight what needs to be changed or to celebrate what is being done well. Most brands realize that an excellent public image is essential if people are going to keep buying their products, so they tend to be quick in addressing any public challenge that reflects badly on the brand.

Spread The Word

Even if you're not a YouTube star with a following in the tens or even hundreds of thousands, you can still spread the word through your use of social media:

 Spread the word via your own social-media presence.

 Affiliate and associate with brands whose environmental manifesto you agree with.

 Start a blog, or comment favourably on planet-saving blogs written by others.

 Join and support communities; this can be as simple as following accounts on Instagram or Twitter.

 Follow hashtags that matter to you.

 Share your own green activities online.

 Become informed (through reading this book!) and share what you have learned.

 Set an example; change your own behaviours and challenge others (gently!) to consider doing the same.

Become passionate about this issue!

Sign petitions urging corporations or governments to make policy changes that will either benefit the environment or put an end to eco-unfriendly practices.

Read books! Watch documentaries! Tag authors and documentary makers; show you have taken their message on board. Then share the message.

CONCLUSION

It's important to acknowledge that **any efforts to be environmentally friendly are meaningful**, but that sometimes we can only do our best. For most of society, there is so much emphasis on being good that adding environmental consciousness can feel like a stretch too far. It comes down to personal choice. Any impetus to change your habits allies itself with the principle of minimalism, which is to simplify your life, your consumption and your use of everything you come into contact with. The beauty of a minimal life is not only that it will **help slow down damage to the planet**; it will also lead to feelings of well-being that are now better understood in the area of human mental health. It's widely accepted that helping others is a good way to bolster feelings of well-being, so committing to a planet-friendly lifestyle is likely to have a similar effect!

Our awareness of the state of the environment comes through a variety of sources, some of which might lead us to think that little can be done. But at this stage in our evolution, **it's crucial we don't give up hope!** It may feel that humans are on a collision course with catastrophe, resulting in the destruction of our planet's precious resources and us with them. It can feel hopeless, especially if we immerse ourselves in a gloomy diet of media reports and alarmist documentaries. But in going green there is something inherently positive, a feeling of goodness, order and harmony akin to opening windows on a sunny day. This feeling shouldn't be ignored but nurtured, as this is what will drive you to **make green endeavours a central, ongoing aspect of your life**, rather than a short-term fad.

Sometimes, of course, it can all seem too much. We grow tired of trying to save the planet; we allow ourselves to be persuaded that the frightening predictions of climate breakdown are far in the future, while the effort to change our ways in the present is exhausting. Naturally, perhaps only semi-consciously, we may wish to take the easy option.

There can indeed be a lot of hand-wringing about the state of the planet by those who care about it most, and it's important to keep a sense of perspective and **make the best endeavours we can**. Conceptually, we know that taking measures to halt damage to the environment should be a priority, but sometimes it can't be – at least, not every day.

In time, though, with the steps outlined in this book and those you can glean from like-minded thinkers, the effort involved will get easier as, out of necessity, the green lifestyle becomes the norm. Retailers will start to understand that their role in supplying goods to us includes environmental responsibility. This is where the activism is so important; if we no longer accept heavily packaged goods, agitate about recycling, exert lobby power through charities and focus groups, and tell governments and corporations we want change, then **change will come**.

You've already made the first step by buying this book, and every other little change you make will help alleviate the pressures that humankind has put on the earth for so long. Together we can start to change the way we shop, eat, travel and recycle, and above all the way we treat Mother Nature. Together we can bring about larger changes by starting a bigger conversation. **Together we can save the world**.

FURTHER READING

Books

Berners-Lee, Mike, *How Bad Are Bananas?: The Carbon Footprint of Everything* (2011)

Clarke, Elanor, *The Little Book of Veganism* (2015)

Dyer, Harriet, *Say No to Plastic* (2018)

Dyer, Harriet, *The Little Book of Going Green* (2018)

Dyer, Harriet, *Say No to Waste* (2019)

Flannery, Tim, *Atmosphere of Hope: Solutions to the Climate Crisis* (2015)

Goodell, Jeff, *The Water Will Come: Rising Seas, Sinking Cities, and the Remaking of the Civilized World* (2017)

Hawken, Paul (ed.), *Drawdown: The Most Comprehensive Plan Ever Proposed to Reverse Global Warming* (2017)

Henson, Robert, *The Rough Guide to Climate Change* (2011)

Klein, Naomi, *This Changes Everything* (2015)

Lynas, Mark, *Six Degrees: Our Future on a Hotter Planet* (2008)

Peters, Jo, *Vegan Life* (2019)

Raygorodetsky, Gleb, *The Archipelago of Hope: Wisdom and Resilience from the Edge of Climate Change* (2017)

Siegle, Lucy, *Turning the Tide on Plastic: How Humanity (And You) Can Make Our Globe Clean Again* (2018)

Documentaries

Earthlings (2005)

An Inconvenient Truth (2006)

Cowspiracy (2014)

The True Cost (2015)

Before the Flood (2016)

An Inconvenient Sequel: Truth to Power (2017)

Chasing Coral (2017)

What the Health (2017)

Drowning in Plastic (2018)

Websites

climate.nasa.gov

eco-age.com

ecobricks.org

energysavingtrust.org.uk

fashionrevolution.org

friendsoftheearth.uk

goodenergy.co.uk

greenchoices.org

greenpeace.org.uk

how-to-save-water.co.uk

onegreenplanet.org

wasteaid.org.uk

If you're interested in finding out more about our books, find us on Facebook at **Summersdale Publishers** and follow us on Twitter at **@Summersdale**.

www.summersdale.com

IMAGE CREDITS